The Girl of Many Colors

Written by Marci Renée

Illustrated by Layken Davey

Copyright © 2023 by Marci Renée

All rights reserved. Published by The Cultural Story-Weaver.

No part of this publication may be reproduced in whole or in part, or stored in a retrieval system, or transmitted in any form or by any means, electronic, mechanical, photocopying, recording, or otherwise, without written permission of the publisher. For information regarding permission, contact The Cultural Story-Weaver at www.culturalstoryweaver.com.

ISBN: 978-1-956242-17-1

I dedicate this book to my four children and all the other Third Culture Kids (TCKs) around the globe. Your different colors are amazing and unique! Shine them for all to see and courageously share them with others. You make this world a more beautiful and more colorful place!

Get Your FREE Coloring Book Here!

www.culturalstoryweaver.com

Sophia was born with two colors.

Her mother was from the United States, so Sophia was blue—like her. Her papa was from France, so Sophia was also orange—like him.

Sophia liked to eat American pancakes with sticky maple syrup like her mother, but she also liked to flip French crêpes and eat them with Nutella like her papa.

"I love my two colors—blue and orange!"

But Sophia sometimes wondered, "Why do I look different from everyone else? They have only one color, but I have two."

When Sophia moved to Senegal, she spoke Wolof, rode a donkey cart in the outdoor market, drank sweet bissap juice, and played fun rhythms on the djembé drum.

Little by little, the purple of Senegal became a part of her. Sophia's colors began to change.

"I love my three colors—blue, orange, and purple!"

But Sophia sometimes wondered, "Why do I look different from everyone else? They have only one color, but I have three."

When Sophia's family moved to Germany, she spoke German, ate big, fat pretzels and sausages, and rode her bike everywhere.

Little by little, the yellow of Germany became a part of her. Sophia's colors began to change.

"I love my four colors—blue, orange, purple, and yellow!"

But Sophia sometimes wondered, "Why do I look different from everyone else? They have only one color, but I have four."

When Sophia moved to Spain, she spoke Spanish, ate churros and chocolate, watched the bulls race through the streets, and danced to the flamenco music.

Little by little, the red of Spain became a part of her. Sophia's colors began to change.

She danced and sang. "I love my five colors—
blue, orange, purple, yellow, and red!"

But Sophia sometimes wondered, "Why do I look different from everyone else? They have only one color, but I have five."

When Sophia's family moved to Morocco, she spoke Arabic, rode camels in the desert, drank sweet mint tea, and ate couscous with her hands.

Little by little, the green of Morocco became a part of her. Sophia's colors began to change.

"I love my six colors—blue, orange, purple, yellow, red, and green!"

But Sophia sometimes wondered, "Why do I look different from everyone else? They have only one color, but I have six."

Sophia sat in her bedroom, admiring her many different colors.

She smiled. "I look like a rainbow!"

"I like sticky American pancakes, but I also like yummy chocolate French crêpes. I like to speak Spanish, but I also like the sounds of Arabic."

"I like to ride my bike, but I also like bumpy donkey carts."

But then, Sophia became sad and confused. She loved her colors, but she didn't understand why she looked different from everyone else.

"I wish I had only one color. I don't want to be different. I want to look like everyone else."

Sophia tried to pull off her colors . . . hide them . . . erase them. But her colors would not go away. They were tightly sewn into her fabric.

"My colors are a part of me . . . forever!"

One day, Sophia met Sarah, a girl of one color.

"I think your rainbow colors are beautiful! Where can I find some?" she asked.

Sophia poured Sarah a glass of sweet, mint tea and made her a big, fat, yummy pretzel. She taught her how to say "bonjour" in French and "adios" in Spanish.

Sophia played her djembé drum and showed Sarah how to flamenco dance. Together, they rode a bumpy camel in the desert.

"Look, Sarah, your colors are changing!" Sophia said.

Sarah was from India. She taught Sophia how to say "hello" in Hindi.

They ate chicken tikka masala while they watched a Bollywood dance show. Little by little, the pink of India became a part of Sophia.

"Wow! It's fun to have different colors!" Sophia said.

"And to share them with each other!" Sarah said.

Together, they ran and played, joyfully spinning and sharing their colors. The world magically became a more beautiful and colorful place!

Interactive Guide for Parents and Teachers

1. Use a globe or the map on the following pages to help your child locate where he lives in the world. Then, help your child locate and identify each country where Sophia lived and its color—France, the United States, Senegal, Germany, Spain, Morocco, and India. Have him say or write the name of the countries in the "color key" in the bottom, left-hand corner.

2. Help your child or student reflect on his own life.
—Where were you born? Find that country on the map and give it a color.
—Where are your parents from? What colors represent their countries?
Find those countries and color them on the map.
—Where have you traveled or lived in the world? What colors would describe those countries? Find them on the map and color them.
—What are some of your favorite objects/foods/people/experiences/memories from the country where you were born, your parents' countries, or the countries you have visited in the world?
—In what ways have some of those experiences changed you? How have you adopted their colors like Sophia?
—Have you ever felt different than the people around you—like Sophia? How did that make you feel?

—What have you done to try to remove your colors or blend in with the people around you?
—Who in your life might be interested in your many different colors and your adventure stories from around the world?
—How could you share your colors and your stories with that person or with others in your family, your school, your neighborhood, etc.?

3. Have your child color the template included or draw a picture of himself with all his different colors. Talk about how the colors have become a part of him, "sewn into his fabric." Encourage your child to celebrate his beautiful colors and to share them with others! Display the coloring page for all to see!

4. Visit the "Kids" section at https://culturalstoryweaver.com/kids/ for coloring pages and cultural stories for kids and adults. Sign up for "Let's Weave Cultures News"!

5. Sign up your child to be "Pen Pals With Sophia." Email her at theculturalstoryweaver@culturalstoryweaver.com

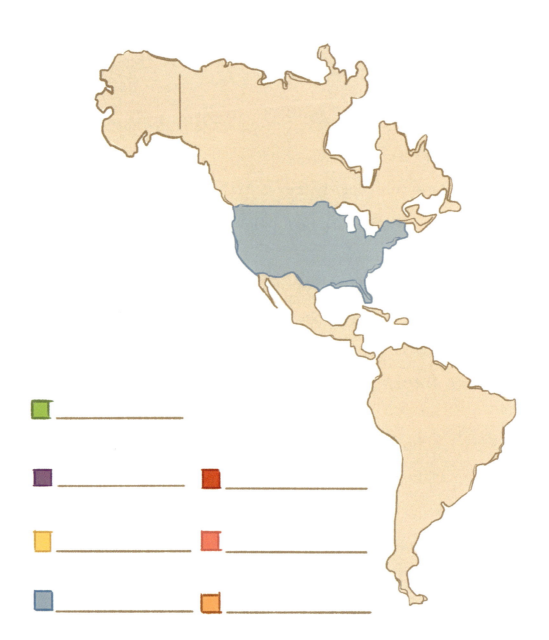

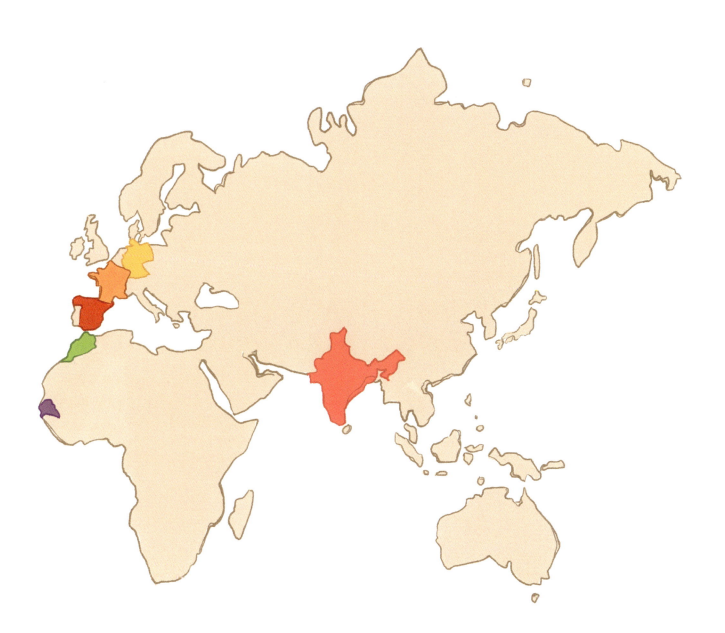

MY COLORFUL ME!

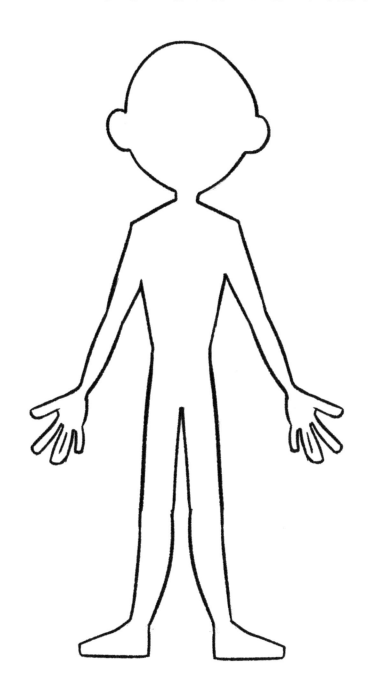

Words From Around the World

Bonjour — Hello (French)
Hola — Hello (Spanish)
Guten tag — Hello (German)
Salaam — Peace/Hello (Arabic)
Namaste — Hello (Hindi)
Gracias — Thank you (Spanish)
Mangi dem — Goodbye (Wolof)
Adios — Goodbye (Spanish)

Marci Renée, along with her French husband, four boys, and dog, Samy, is a global nomad, who has traveled to more than thirty countries and has lived overseas in the United States, France, Morocco, and Spain. She loves to travel, speak foreign languages, experience different cultures, eat ethnic foods, meet people from faraway lands, and of course, tell stories. She is the published author of 5 children's books and 4 creative non-fiction memoirs for adults. Visit her at www.culturalstoryweaver.com

Layken Davey was born in South Africa and grew up in Morocco. She loves stories, from anywhere and everywhere, and drawing characters and animals—especially horses. Layken is the illustrator of Marci's other children's picture books. Visit her at www.instagram.com/laykendavey/

Get Your FREE Coloring Book Here!

Discover Marci Renée's other children's books—
The Boy Who Weaves the World
The Boy of Many Colors
My Tower is Tumbling!
Mommy, What's a Safe House?

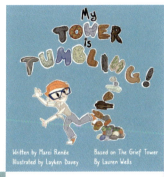
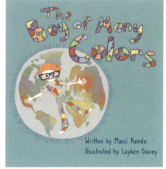
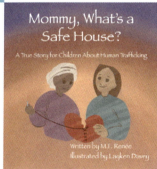

Find all her books at www.culturalstoryweaver.com/books/

SCAN ME

Made in the USA
Middletown, DE
13 June 2023

32298427R00029